MW01592156

POETIC IMAGERY IN MOTION

Presents

PAGES FROM MY HEART

VOL 1

BY

FREDERIQUE MEDIA PRODUCTIONS

FREDERIQUE MEDIA PRODUCTIONS

EBook
ISBN-10: 0988339102
ISBN-13: 978-0-9883391-0-1

Amazon
ASIN: B009VJ3IK0

Softcover
ISBN-10: 0988339110
ISBN-13: 978-0-9883391-1-8

First Edition: December 2012

Poetic Imagery in Motion
http://poeticimageryinmotion.com
http://FrederiqueCapital.com/piim

This book was printed in the United States of America.

Table of Contents

Table of Contents

Part II: Spiritual

Table of Contents

Part III: Spoken Words

Table of Contents

Part IV: *Author's Notes*

Table of Contents

ACKNOWLEDGMENTS

As a man who has been driven to live a life filled with purpose, it gives me great pleasure to acknowledge the one who gave it to me in the first place, God. Since I was young, I recognized that you gave me multiple skills and multiple gifts. I want to thank you for entrusting me with these talents so that the world can be inspired by your greatness. For I know the plans that you have in store for me. I am just a vessel being led by your will to create and bless others.

It has taken me over twelve years to bring this book to life. But I truly understand that everything happens in God's time not mine. In doing so, I have met my wife Suzanne S. Frederique who has been a great supporter in getting this book of poems published. Thank you for your understanding and unwavering love and devotion to our dreams. Thank you for believing in me when others did not.

Aside from my wife, Linda K. Johnson has been a great support and a friend in her encouragement to write this book in the first place. Thank you for listening over these past few years as I spoke to you tirelessly time after time about my dreams. You have always proven to be more than just a business friend over the years. We have shared a lot of stories as well as memories over the years. Thank you for playing a part in achieving this milestone with me.

We have all heard the saying that patience is a virtue. Well I really could not have gotten to this point in my life if I did not wait for two very important technologies to develop in those twelve years. The concept of on demand publishing and eBooks did not exist twelve years ago. Therefore the vision that I had for publishing this book would not have been possible had I not waited. Now that statement is even more relevant for the woman that came into my life two years ago. The best way to describe her role in helping me finish this book is to say this. There is a point and time in your life that God will put someone in your life for a season and a reason that may not be known to you. But when the time comes that person will show up unexpectedly. Evelyn D. Robinson has been such a blessing to my life for the past two years as she gave me insight, direction, and taught me so much about publishing my first eBook. And it would not have been at all possible if she too did not learn the necessary *"Lessons"* by her mother Dolores E. Pickett who authored her first book recently. Evelyn, thank you so much for allowing me to follow the tracks that you have laid out for me. You are truly the epitome of the phrase, "a candle loses nothing when it lights another candle." Thank you for all of your editorial support and the countless hours of late night phone calls. I could not have done this without your undying support.

Part I

Love Poems

Seeking Soulmate

Young Poet, Philosopher early 20s
Seeks a lover and a friend,
A companion:

Intellectually strong and Independent
Is what I seek in you.

Compassionate and sweet
Are the qualities you must meet.

Educated,
Open minded,
Conservative,
Free spirited,
Is what I am and what I seek

Courageous and loving,
Skin deep,
Is what will win my heart.

Lonely and bored,
I await your call.

Desperate I must look,
You say,
To be searching for you
Through the personals.

What a fool I must be
With all this in mind.

Reading the morning paper
To find my soul's desire

Days go by
I sit and read
Sipping coffee has been my routine.

Expecting to find you,
I must be dreaming!

Get up and Get dressed!
Is the only way I will find
The soul-mate I seek.

The Heavens Above

The first time I laid my eyes on you,
You took my breath away.
I was speechless and overwhelmed by your beauty.
My heart was electrified with the fear and uncertainty that it could be you
Lurking before me when I least expected it to be you.

You took me by surprise
As you shine your pearls of beauty in the darkness.
Like The Heavens Above, you glimmer
As you masquerade into the different constellations
In the imagination of those who gazed upon you.

You put me in a daze as I stand and watch you from above.
Your beauty is beyond all that is beautiful.
Words alone cannot describe your presence.
To speak of you in human words, would be unjustified!

If there ever was such a thing as a miracle in the world,
May I wish to touch thee upon my looking glass
So that I may know how thou feel with thy beauty nearby.
The touch of thy presence at heart will rest my soul a thousand fold to sleep.

My love,
Do not be jealous
As I look at the beauty each gem of nebula has to offer,
For my love is universal.

Though separated by day,
 I long to see you in the darkness.
As I await your first sign,
Our hearts beat eons between Heaven and Earth in earnest.

Love, I leave you with this in mind:
If you ever miss me while we are apart,
Just look at the stars above and
You will know that I will be looking at you
From The Heavens Above.

Have You Ever...

Made love (to a woman) so much that she cried.

Made love (to a woman) with your eyes
Only to see the glimmer of light so bright as a star shining through a prism
Only to see that which is a reflection of her beauty.

Made love (to a woman) in your mind that it hurts so much
But all you can do is rest your fragile heart to a pillow.

Made love (to a woman) so much that she could not even walk after
Only the smooth touch of a hot bubble bath
Or the pulsing jets of a hot tub that reminds you of him deep inside of you
Is the only thing that could cool you down.

Made passionate love (to a man) so much that you knew he was the one
The one and only one you've been waiting for
The one that shall even be your friend, lover, confidant.
Yeah, that one
The one that keeps you awake at night missing his presence
Even the smell of his body in your arms.

Loved a man so much that his touch alone can make you come
Come from the slightest touch of his hands in your arms
The touch of his hands stroking your hair
The touch of his body, his chess so muscular and handsome
The touch of his butt cheeks in your hands
The touch of his arms, so strong and manly or even
The touch of his fingers slowly caressing your back
Stroking you up and down
As if he had magical fingers
That can penetrate the inside of your vagina and up to your clitoris.

Been kissed so passionately that the taste of his lips is forever in your mind
Days, weeks, months, or even years may have passed by
But the slight touch or smell of his lips next to yours
Can bring back the sensation of when you last made love.

Seen the resemblance of his shadow for a moment in the darkness
Or even hear the crackling steps he makes as he enters the house
Only to have awaken the sexual pheromones that keeps you dripping wet for no reason
Yet, his mere appearance in your mind has caused you to uncontrollably climax
As if, you no longer have control of your own body.

Made passionate love (to a man) so much but only to feel empty inside

Cause you knew he was never yours to keep in the first place.

Fallen in love with that married man or woman you knew was wrong
But your love is so strong that you would even bear his child.

Made love so good that when you climax deep within him
All you can do is just cry with joy
As you give birth to such a precious life
That the date of conception has never left you.

Found the one I've been speaking of
The one that comforts you
Gives you the security you need
The one that even shares the same passion as you
But only to sleep next to that man, woman, or even your spouse
Who is not the one.

Stopped for a moment to think about him
Even to think about why?
Why does he give you goose bumps
Or even put a smile on your face when you think of his name
Or even see his manly presence.

Wondered about that guy or gal that just walked by you
S/he was so HOT
But you never made the first move
Only to wonder,
What if …
As you stare out into space

What if,
You ask yourself, he was the one at this very second in time
Should I have said a word, a whisper at least
To let 'em know that … that … Ahhhhhh.

What if these memories I spoke of was only to be desired by you
Yes, you,
The one I have allowed to slip away.

Have You Ever loved?
I have, so why haven't you?

Lady in the Shadow

I have dreamt of you since I was a teenage boy.
But my love for you was not that of a childish fantasy.
I felt your touch and warmth as a man should love a woman as beautiful as you.
Therefore, are you not my wife that hides in the shadow?

Was I not the man of your dreams?
Better yet, your one true love, you've been waiting for?
Are you not the one that I have walked a thousand miles
Across the land and the sea searching for?

I remembered you, as if it was yesterday that I felt your sweet embrace in my bed.
So, have we met before, Lady in the Shadow?
I have made love to you before but only in the shadow.
Lady, I have always dreamt of making passionate love to you
But only in the shadow.
So, why do you hide in my shadow?

I have touched your body and kissed your very lips.
I have seen myself penetrating your very soul.
I have suckled on your very breast
And have been aroused by your voluptuous thighs,
Wrapped around my legs, as you drip your orgasmic love juice on the sheets.
Our hearts were inseparable as if yoked into one.

It was this very love that birth our first and only child together.
For a moment, time stood still
As I felt the tear drops down my face
For I knew this was our forbidden love.

So why can't I ever see your face in my dreams?
Are you not the soul mate I have been waiting for?
So than, why do you hide away from me?

My fair lady,
I beg to ask you once again;
Are you, the Lady in the Shadow?

Love Potion # 8

You say your man has left you, well child I have in my kitchen the Love Potion that will win him back for good. Have a seat and take down some notes!

If you ever wanted to mend a broken heart, you need to take a piece of that heart. Now if your man has a good heart or a bad one, here are your options.

First you need to take that heart of his out of his body. To do so take a sharp knife and cut along the edges of his left chest. (if unsure of location, see the fast rhythmic pounding of his chest as he sees the sharp glare of the knife coming at him on the table.)

Next, gently pull out its members until you can see the heart beating in the palm of your hand.

Now slowly squeeze the blood out of his heart and into a pot. (Make sure to leave a few drops of blood so the heart can function again once inside the body.)

Second, to get your man back, you have one of many options. Take from one or all of the following recipes if needed.

Loyalty — *for the unfaithful one who can't stop cheating.*

Honesty — *for the one who can't tell you the truth without leaving a smile after each sentence.*

Respect — *for the one who thinks you should be on your hands and knees.*

The Stray Dog — *for the one who can't find a mate but manage to hop around.*

The Lazy one — *for the one who can't get a stable job or can't lift a thing in the house. Basically, the bum. You get my drift.*

Each ingredient contains a special spell which can be found only in Mama's kitchen. Not no convenient store like the 7-11 you here!

Third, add 2 drops of tears (don't poke the eye too much, 2 drops is enough) and a pinch of salt to give it that special flavor, than mix it up for that final taste.

Here it stands before you Love Potion #8, the Love Sauce, all disguised in a peace offering super.

Fourth, serve with his favorite dish. Not any old dish but his most favorite. That way he can't resist but to come on over.

Invite him over to make amends with the intent of becoming civil friends. Wine and dine him with an everlasting memory.

Fifth, give or take 2 to 4 hours for actual effect. Then you shall discover the rebirth of the man of your dreams.

If all fails, pick from the various Love Potions available and add more.

Disclaimer

1) Several shots of whisky is recommended before commencing Love Potion #8. 2) Take caution, for a good man, I recommend a few drops here and there for a better result. 3) Not liable for death, lawsuits, or manslaughter charges that may occur in any future event from using this or any other Love Potions.

Lost Love

We live to learn and mistakes we shall make.
But only through experience and time
Would we learn to forgive the one we had loved dearly.

I can only hope in time that all ruins shall be mended
So that love can shine upon us.
For time is short and each waking day that pass us by
I dream of you smiling back at me.

We may not work to those who love not
But I cannot help to think of the possibilities
Had we conquered our fears and fought the odds.
What tales could have been said about thee?

For our children's children would have shared the tale
Of what true love is all about?
A legacy would have been left
From the ventures we par take through our hearts' desire.

Even though time has kept us apart
Remember, true love is meant to last,
I hope yours will last for all eternity
For my love for you has proven the test of time.

Mistakes can be forgiven in time but
Love cannot regain the time lost in between.
But my heart will wait for the lifetime it shall take
To see the Amber in your eyes smiling back at me once again.

For I will always love you, for all Eternity...

Ode to an Apple

An ellipse not perfect but round.

Reminds one of the fruits of temptation

So divine and sweet

Plump yet not ripe.

From the shadows of the light, it glares.

Its top like that of a black hole

Pulsating in rhythm with each beat of your heart

Ready to suck you in.

Its body soft and smooth

Leaving only a few bumps to symbolize its imperfections.

Its skin green with deception

While beauty lurks within.

The aroma of sweetness

Waiting to sip out at the slight of a bite.

The temptation,

Hard to resist.

As you open her up,

Taste the juice she releases

As you penetrate

The center of her core.

In the end,

You lick your fingers

After you ate her hole.

Hoping to capture all she had to offer,

You prey around craving for more.

That which was beauty in your eyes is now satisfaction to your stomach!

When We First Made Love

When We First Made Love,
I knew you were a blessing
From the Heavens Above,

The way you touch me girl was a feeling of ecstasy.
As I open my heart to you,
You cured all my wounds with your tender kiss,
As I lay down and close my eyes,
I can still feel your body next to mine,
As I dream of When We First Made Love.

Never again shall a woman make me feel the same way as you,
Cause our first will always be unique.

Your beloved lips are tender and sweet,
As we embrace.

Your skin, so soft and gentle,
That of a new born baby
Fresh into a nurtured world.

My arms crests your shoulders up and down,
With a gentle stroke,
As you relax your head next to mine and whisper,
I love you.

The times we've glazed at each other's eyes
Has never been the same as today.

As I stare deep within your eyes
And see the glimmer of your bright blue eyes,

You smiled at me for a moment
And I stopped to give thanks to the Lord,
For you have been a God sent from the Heavens Above.

The lonely days I've waited to make love to you,
While refusing the pleasures from the fruits of temptation
Was a blessing in disguise,
As I hold back
The countless years of tears
That I have shed for you.

Tonite, your disguise has been yet worth the wait
Of endless heartaches and broken promises,
False hopes and expectations.

So why not share these tears
Once again for you, my love.
For they are tears of joy
And that not of sorrow.

There is No One Else like You

When I open my eyes and think of you
All I have to do is look in the mirror and I see your reflection in me
And these are the words that define my love.

You are my strength,
My undying love.
You are my hope,
My future.

You are my sistha in Christ.
You are my confident,
My soulmate.

There is No One Else like You

For you were made for me and only me!
You are my destiny that I have waited for so long to come and complete me.
You are my right hand.

There is No One Else like You

For there is no other woman like you!
You are my queen, the mother of my unborn children.
You breathe life into my soul.

For I can't help myself
Cause I am so lost without you by my side.
You are the rock, that keeps me steady and focus.
You are the woman that steers my sail.

How does it feel to know that I am unworthy of your love?

Cause, There is No One Else like You

Like a lion who seeks out his prey
With a keen sense of smell,
A pinpoint sense of sight, &
A superb sense of hearing,
I too seek out my mate with the same passion.

For God took his time to create a Diva such as you.
From the very first thought of your creation
To the birth of your existence,
God knew that you will be admired by all men who cross your path.

For you are the envy of all women
Who stands in your presence.
You are the epitome of all brothers
Who can stand to be blessed by your side.

From afar,
The aroma of your beauty is ever lasting.
As I await your approach,
I can see the essence of God's creation lurking in the shadows
As the hot summer sun draws her image on the very ground she walks on.

As if the goddess of Love and Beauty,
Aphrodite was praising the very earth she walks on.

My senses have heightened.
I am alert and attentive to her very footsteps.
I can feel the very blood of my veins rushing through my body with anticipation.
My muscles, intensify with adrenaline
Like a lion prepares for the chase of his life.

My eyes are focus on her every movement,
Combing through for any signs of weakness.
There is none to be seen.
For her stature is divine and perfectly made by the Holy One.
For I know it will be the toughest fight of my life to win her love.

From the top to the bottom
I see the perfection of my black sistha.
I see the natural straight hair of her ancestors that was passed on by birth,
Which accentuate her chocolate covered skin from being damaged by the sun.

Her face is so strong
By the definition of her facial expressions
That fear come upon thy,
"If you get out of line and don't come correct."

Her brown eyes glow with delight and shine
So bright that you can see the innocent within.
Nevertheless her eyebrows are thick and firm,
To give you that look,
"Mama don't play that!"
Her thick nose reminds you that a true African queen awaits you.

Her strong cheekbone tells you of the ancestral hardship she had endured for centuries.

Her lips so thick and succulent due to the years she had to remain silent behind the man.

Still her voice remained silent until she had the right to vote.

But in all she can kill you with her charm and her beautiful smile.

Her shoulders so strong and thick
Like her arms which had to bear the tiers of many weeping men from slavery.
She took on arms to protect her own family,
Even raised that picket sign high with pride to end segregation.

She bore the burdens of many men who lacked the strength to provide for their family.
All of the ones who chose to walk away from their responsibility as a father.
She took on the chore of taking out the trash each week.

She even took on the strength
To take care of the house and work outside of the home
When you went to war to fight for our freedom.

Her bosoms are so voluptuous yet firm at times of need.
For every weeping man shall cry into the comfort of the bosom of a strong black woman.
For all men will find inner peace once again
As they stare in wonder as to why
It takes a village to raise a family?

Her full figured waste line and wide hips
Are there to mesmerize your every thought as she pass you by.
Her stride back and forth in your mind
Will make you never forget that she is ready to bear your child.
That she has become a woman
That is prepared to nurture your first born
Into existence without any worry of miscarriage.
That she is indeed a woman, mature, and ready
To enter into an adult relationship with you.

Last but not least her thick thighs so strong and elegant.
She has walked many miles alone without you.
Yet she too had to walk many miles in your shadow
As she stayed firm to her morals and values.

As she grew stronger and stronger waiting for you to lead your household,
She became that strong independent woman that some men became afraid of.
For she has already walked her own path in the shadows of men but now she walks in the
Footsteps of millions of black women of color who have walked this Earth.

Therefore I stand on the shoulders of many great black women
Who have passed before me.
Who have fought a good fight
So that I can stand before you.

Now as she stands before me in passing
It brings me great joy to hear her speak with all the elegance that is her beauty.
Her chosen words speaks well of her intellectual delight.
For she is balanced in all that God has created for me.

Therefore when I look at that mirror and put on that sharp business suit,
I know that I stand firm behind the shadow
Of a strong black woman who had given birth to me.

For without her by my side,
I am as weak as the next man.

Hence

There is No One Else like You!

Your Eyes Told Me

I knew it all along from the look in your eyes cause
Your Eyes Told Me

I knew you were the one I would fall deeply in love with cause
Your Eyes Told Me

From the depth of my heart to the edge of my soul cause
Your Eyes Told Me

I knew this friendship would last forever cause
Your Eyes Told Me

I knew that I had found my better half cause
Your Eyes Told Me

From the first touch of your lips to the first time we made love cause
Your Eyes Told Me

I knew it was true love cause
Your Eyes Told Me

I knew you were the one I would spend the rest of my life with cause
Your Eyes Told Me

I knew you were the one who shall bear my first child cause
Your Eyes Told Me

From each day that past by to each breath that I take
Every day of the week I knew cause
Your Eyes Told Me

I knew that I was ready to commit to one person for the rest of my life cause
Your Eyes Told Me

I knew that I was safe in your arms, that you will never break my heart cause
Your Eyes Told Me

For Your Eyes Told Me
Together we are bonded as one, for all eternity
For I knew I would ask you on this day,
Would You Marry Me!
Cause Your Eyes Told Me so!

Part II

Spiritual

Thank You Lord

The years you have stood beside me
Truly speaks well of your name, Father.

You have been with me
From the start to the end.

From my struggles
To my happiness
You have been there.

You never once let me down
Through the test of hardship,
Yet I have let you down many times.

I could always count on you
To get me through my troubles
When I lost hope.

The countless times you have bailed me out
When I called out to you,
You never once asked much of me in return.

Selfish I have been
Throughout these years,

Taking for granted the love
You have shown to all your children.

All I could say is,
Thank You Lord.

For all the good and the bad
We have done,

You still found space in your heart
To love each one of us.
There have been times when we did not
Deserve to call you, our Father.

For the things we have done with your name
And at times in your name.

We have been a selfish race of humans
For the hatred we have spread with your name

For the bombs we have dropped,
The wars we have lived through,
The blood we have shed,
With the hands that have praised you.

The same ones which has made the sign
Of the cross and even with the lips
That once praised your name with honor
But now has lost the faith.

For the times we have been heartless
And neglected our fellow brothers and sisters.
I thank you, from the bottom of our hearts.

Most of all, I thank you for taking my hands
As your child, guiding me through each step
Of life's journeys.

I want to Thank You Lord,
For allowing me to love.
For giving me many second chances
When I did not deserve it.

For these things, I love you.

The Four Seasons

Winter

Mother Nature must rest and sleep.
For a new day is coming.

Spring

New life is planted in the rich soil.
For the harvest to come.

Summer

Is the celebration of life's abundance.
For it is the fruit of our labor.

Fall

Is the renewing of life.
For a cleansing of what was once old is new again

That's True Love

I believe it to be True Love.
That together we are bonded as one, for all eternity.
For our souls are connected as one beyond the life that we live.

Did you forget that we are attached at the hip?
Didn't you know that I cannot live without you in my life?
Didn't you know how hurt I would be if you left me behind?

When you died, a piece of my heart went with you.
You left me empty inside yearning for one moment in time
To see you smile at me once again.

For my soul is unstable just watching you laying there.
For am I to accept that this is the last time I shall ever see you again?

How can I go on to an empty house and pretend that it's going to be ok.
When the world never knew you the way that I loved you.

Do you not understand how deep my love is?
For they may not understand what True Love is all about.
For when I said I do, it was till death do us apart.
So I cannot say goodbye for I am not ready to let go.

Life goes on, hang in there, stay strong,
It's gonna be ok, God be with you, is what I've been told.
As if it will stop my pain.

We can plan it, we can think of it, for those who are brave.
But in the end, we are never ready to say goodbye.
For every man on Earth, our time will come too.

You can deny it all you want, you can be as rich as the next man,
And you can even try to play God in the lab,
But all the Earthly goods that you possess can never buy your way out of time.

But when the time comes you must ask yourself this,
Did you love your man like I did?

Did you take care of him like you should?
Did you say that I love you each day?
Did you ever hold him in your arms and look deep in his eyes
But you said it without a sound from your lips?

But before I go,
Remember this,
Don't have too much fun without me in heaven.
For it won't be too long before I join you.

That's True Love!
For you will always be my love.

Season's Greetings

Christmas

Is about

Remembering

The most important things in your life.

Sharing memories with family and those that love you dearly.

It's about bringing joy, love,

And prosperity to all families near and far to us.

Children of the Earth,

Always remember that the heart of Christmas is within you and me.

May God bring us closer each year as we search for inner peace and love in a new year.

Hence that time is upon us now, so let us embrace it, for we cannot change the past.

May we leave the old behind and welcome in a new year full of hope, dreams, and life.

But most of all,

Remembering that Jesus is the reason for the season

Which gives us a purpose to rejoice and shout out his holy name.

So give freely of your heart, knowing that a new year is soon upon us.

What lies for us in the New Year is in the hands of God.

So be thankful for the life you have today. For it is God's will that tomorrow comes.

God's fortune and joy was the day he brought you and I into this world we call home.

So cherish the life that you live

As if it was your last breath.

For tomorrow is not promise

Therefore I wish you and your family

A Seasons' Greetings,

A Merry Christmas,

Happy Holidays,

Happy Hanukkah,

Happy Kwanzaa,

Feliz Navidad,

And a Happy New Year!

This Christmas
2007

This Christmas Lord has been a special one.
What else can I ask of you that I have not gotten.
You gave me two beautiful daughters that I love so much.
You gave me a woman for which I adore.
You showed me hope of a brighter tomorrow.
You showed me kindness and happiness that has never been felt before.
You brought me peace on Earth for the first time.
You have given me clarity to go forth in the New Year.
You have opened my eyes so that I can see your vision for me.
You have declared This Christmas to be a new day for my breakthrough.
You have not forgotten me through my struggles even when I lost hope for a better
tomorrow.

You showed the world mercy upon my soul when I was down on my luck.
This Christmas I celebrate you and give thanks for forsaking your only Son, our God.
You are my salvation. You are my one and true God. I shall not forget you This Christmas.

Let not I never forget the things I have to be thankful for during this season of giving
Praise to our one true God, our father.

Let not I forget your purpose for breathing life on to my soul as the clock strike twelve and
A new year unfolds onto me.

As I reflect upon my past, deliver me Lord from my pain & suffering and bring on a new
day
For my season has come forth on this day.

It is within This Christmas, my breakthrough shall come.
I have arrived Lord for this day, This Christmas, my time has come.

I will breathe life onto your words.
I will preach your Gospel on to death ears so that they may hawk your message.

I will lead them Lord to your Promise Land. For I have seen my destiny clear as the sunrise
Over the mountain top.

Lord, you have set me free. *I wise* for I am free!
Free at last, Free at last,
Thank God almighty, I am Free at last!

AMEN

The Last Sunset:
An Ode to Lyon Heart

The sun rises,

The sun sets,

The moon rises & sets many times.

But today the heart of the sun no longer rises.

The Lyon has fought a long battle full of pain, memories, and broken hearts.

The day has come when the Lyon must rest.

He has seen many sun rises which symbolize

The beginning of day and the start of life.

The Lyon has also seen many sunsets which symbolize

The end of day and the end of life itself.

The battle is over and the Lyon has lost the battle against the plague,

But the plague continues all over in a different host.

The heart of the Lyon is not broken but has grown stronger because he has gone

Beyond the light and men's ability to comprehend.

The Lyon has lived a great life

But has saddened the hearts of the next generation.

For they will never see the Lyon again

But will only have the deem memories of his being.

The dark orange and bright yellow glare reflecting off the ocean,

Is now gone and the Lyon has gone with it.

I once said the plague of the twentieth century is not too far from home,

On that day God proved me right

May the heart of the Lyon rest forever.

In memory of Lyonel Frederique:

Thursday, August 11, 1994

Am I the One?

Lord, what is your purpose for my life?
I have been roaming the land empty hearted for so long.
I have come to accept the truth, I am lost?
I have come to a fork in the road as I stand before you
Pleading for an answer that has been in my heart, Am I the One?

-Where are you, Oh mighty man of God?
-Are you the one who shall deliver me from my wicked ways?
-Are you my end and my beginning?
-Lord, I find myself lost in the world, lost in desire, lost for my passion.
-Am I really a mighty warrior of God's army?

Then the Lord answers my cry.

-If you think you are not the one, then the devil is ready for you.
-For he has a spot for all who are weak and do not know their place in my kingdom.
-I have set you apart at birth. But you rejected me.
-I have forsaken the weakness in your bloodline,
-So you can stand strong and lead my people.
-I have broken the yoke that has held you back.
-For you are the chosen one.

-Do you not know who you are?
-I gave you those visions in your dreams.
-For I know why I created you.
-Your pain and sorrow is not for my amusement.
-For I know who you are and what you will become.

-Lord, do you believe a wretch like me can be called to serve your army of believers?
-Am I the One to lead God's people?
-Am I ready to lead them after 33 years in the wilderness?
-Am I prepared to fight God's fight?
-No, not me Lord! You must be mistaken!

And Jesus responded, yes son, I want to use you just as you are.

-This is a new millennium. I have given you a fresh start.
-2008 is the year of new beginnings.
-If there was a time to begin something new, this is the year to do it.
-Your destiny has already been laid out for you.
-You just have to start living out those dreams that I have put forth before you.

Lord, if it is your will:

-Cleanse my spirit new so that I may see the future that you have in store for me.
-Lord I will give you my heart; I will give you my soul. Just show me the way.
-I will not fear. For my heart is filled with your love
-For I know my place in your kingdom now.
-When I am asked, Who Am I? I will not fear because I am a mighty man of God.
-When it is all said and done,
-Ain't none but Jesus who was crucified to set me free.

This is where it ends and eternity starts for me.

Unborn Love

Words cannot express the loss of a loved one, let alone the loss of your unborn child.
How do you begin to express those feelings of anger, pain, and emptiness?
A pamphlet is handed to me titled, "Fathers Grieve Too" for the loss of one's life.
But how do you express in writing the love of your unborn child still in the womb to a stranger?

Is it like connecting a face to a name or a person's personality to his or her character?
What about the unknown two months it had been with us but not to a stranger? The joy of planning out its name, the sex, the bedroom colors, whose personality or character will our child have? The emotions that comes with having your first baby or believing you have done everything right by God's commandments until this very day. Can it all be explained or expressed within this pamphlet that was handed to me?

I still believed that my baby would be ok. I prayed to God for hope and strength that what I was growing through was only a figment of my imagination.
From the early morning spotting in her panties, I denied it in God's holily name
To the contractions she was having on the ride to the hospital I felt helpless. The moaning, stomach cramps, screaming, and crying all left me paralyzed in agony not knowing what else can I do to comfort my newly bride. Only in God I sought comfort again, only to ask why can I not carry the pain she bears for a short moment while our baby lies there in peace? As if being a man meant I can endure more pain than the generations of women before her who have given birth to a new born.

I still believe I said to myself watching in disbelief as I looked at the ultrasound of my baby laying there. A strong boy with a smile is what I saw as she holds my hands in tears. I thought I saw a smiling baby only two months in my mind's eye letting me know that he will be strong, for he is a healthy Frederique.

The results are in and the "Uterus is cleared out" were the words I thought I heard out of the nurse's mouth. Like a foreign language was spoken to me, I stood still awaiting the good news. Yet not a tear was shed cause I still believed in my Unborn Love. Denial may have set in but the reality was soon to come as a loved one called over the phone, and I said to her "she miscarried." Not a tear was still shed until I heard the voice, "repeat it again," that I felt the raindrops. For I have lost my unborn child on a beautiful but sunny fall day.

An hour had past and a quiet ride home it is. Disbelief has set in again. For it was all over with just a pull and a tug. Through the specula came out the placenta and her pain had stopped. Yet two hours ago, I knew my wife bared a life in her womb. Shall I tell her a joke to put a smile on her face? For it has been my role as a father and a husband to make sure she is always happy and safe. What else is there to do for the day is still young? Shall we pretend and carry on as life deemed us to do? Or will a baby passing by wake us to reality and say why did you let me go? Or should we move on without fear that it was God's will not ours to bear life once again to term?

Knocking on Heaven's Door

It's a beautiful Saturday morning.
The sun is shining brightly upon heavens' door.
The sky is radiant with spots of sunlight
Blasting through the clouds
Like a beacon calling the dead home.

We have lost another family member.
And at any given time of day,
God will call a loved one home.

And there it is,
Another knock on the door.
Someone is Knocking on Heavens' Door
Asking to come in
Just to be with the Lord.

The older we get as children,
The further apart we seem to grow from each other.
And a new life is born.

But a good old home coming
Always brings us back to each other's arms.
To a welcome embrace that was long overdue.

It's as if each Knock on Heavens' Door,
There is a celebration
To rekindle old friendships,
To reunite loved ones,
And mend old broken hearts over the years.

God,
Is it all part of your designed plan,
To bring us one step closer to you Lord?
To seek your purpose
And remember who is King of all kings,
And the Lord of all lords?

For you are the beginning and the end.
The Alpha and the Omega.
You see the light before the darkness.

So it is ok to ask God in times of sorrow
What is the purpose of life?
Better yet, what is God's purpose in your life?
What is the significance of my life?
What is your intended purpose for my life?
What is your divine purpose for my existence?

My child,
All of those questions will be answered
The day you Knock on Heavens' Door.
We are all scheduled to come back home,
At any given point in time.

Until then,
God will be waiting and listening patiently
For the day you Knock on Heaven's Door.

-My Eulogy -
Please Read in My Absence

In the event that I am not here,
I want to say farewell.
I want to leave my dear loved ones with some parting words.

And for those who may not have the pleasure to know of thee,
Let me enlighten you on the life that was once my own to live.

It has always been my dream to see you all at my home coming party.
Know that I am here with you all on borrowed time
Just so I can get to see a glimpse of the crowd at my own funeral.

I have always believed
Just the sheer amount of people
Here today to bear witness to my life

Lets me know that I had lived a life
Filled with significance,
Filled with love, and
One that had a purpose.

Your presence here alone confirms that.
It also represents a foot print,
Stamped in time of the impact
I had in each one of your lives.

I may not always be there to lead the way
But I hope that I have set you on the right path
Towards your purpose
& destiny.

I will forever remember
Your friendships,
Your love,
And the memories we had together.

Upon my untimely death,
I had hope my tombstone would read
Like a resume of accomplishments.

Here lived a man who was defined by his principles,
Code of conduct,
Morales,
& Ethics.

A man of God,
A man for others,
A man of integrity,
A father & a husband.

An Entrepreneur,
A philosopher,
A philanthropist.

A man of vision,
A futurist,
A poet,
A writer.

May these be the words that shall forever be engraved on my tombstone.
May they also be an ever lasting legacy in the hearts of those I've touched for all eternity.

May God bless you all!

Part III

Spoken Words

Who Am I

Who Am I
When I was just an egg in my mother's womb?
Who Am I
When I was born into slavery?
Am I just 3/4 of a person?
Who Am I
Seconds before I was born?
Who Am I
Before I was named?

Who Am I,
I am Dimitry Frederique.
I am unique
Who Am I,
I am an intellectual man.
Who Am I,
I am an educator.
Who Am I,
I am the greatest.
Who Am I,
I am the forgotten.
Who Am I,
I am the unknown.
Who Am I,
I am the pride & tears of joy from my mother's eyes.

Who Am I,
I am spiritual.
Who Am I,
I am a leader.
Who Am I,
I am a human being.
Who Am I,
I am great & beautiful
Who Am I,
I am the oppressed.
Who Am I,
I am the hope.
Who Am I,
I am the future.
Who Am I,
I am a child of God.
Who Am I,
I am the dream of Dr. Martin Luther King's, " I have a dream "

Who Am I,
I am destined for greatness.
Who Am I,
I am the chosen one.
Who Am I,
I am the peace maker.
Who Am I,
I am the abolitionist.
Who Am I,
I am a scientist, an Astronomer, & a Computer Scientist.

Who Am I,
I am the star that shines brightly in the sky.
Who Am I,
I am compassionate.
Who Am I,
I am talented.
Who Am I,
I am God on the cross.
Who Am I,
I am a Catholic.
Who Am I,
I am the messenger from God.

Who Am I,
I am the loneliness in your eyes.

Who Am I,
I am the poor.
Who Am I,
I am freedom.
Who Am I,
I am an honorable man.
Who Am I,
I am justice.
Who Am I,
I am a dreamer.
Who Am I,
I am a thinker of the 21st century
Who Am I,
I am a renaissance man.
Who Am I,
I am a knight in shining armor.
Who Am I,
I am a man stuck between two worlds.
Who Am I,
I am the heart-broken.
Who Am I,

I am the shattered dreams of a drive-by shooting.

Who Am I,
I am history.
Who Am I,
I am the one million man of the Million Man March.
Who Am I,
I am that dream of the Million Man March.
Who Am I,
I am the big brother and big sister.
Who Am I,
I am a poet.
Who Am I,
I am a biracial child.
Who Am I,
I am the past, present, & future.

Who Am I ?
I am, therefore I am an educated man.
Who are you?

Last but not least,
I am a black man,
A descendent of Haitian & African slaves.
So before you look at my skin color,
Look at my credentials & love me for who I am!

The Eagle

His name tells of how it was with him and those who have passed before him
His name foreign to the western world but well known overseas
Where the great ones once rejected now praised
For their contribution to society

His name carries a legacy of the great scientists
Who have pass beyond the light

Those the likes of Einstein, Copernicus, Galileo, & Newton
And the ones who will remain nameless in history

Heaven knows the vision he brings for the 21st century

Guided by the path of his mentors
His knowledge brings forth wisdom
To those who would listen and learn his ways

A visionary full of life
Determined he is to triumph
Over the obstacles put forth by mankind
Ready to uncover the unknown
That stands beyond our reach
He studies the cosmos
For it is his destiny

A man sensitive and strong
Soft, tenderly & kind, yet fragile like a new born baby
Loving and compassionate is his repertoire

Shy and timid he is
Friendly and helpful define his qualities

For his good deeds, hard work, & dedication
He is spoken highly of by those who know him
Therefore
A place shall be set for him
Next to the Lord

Spiritually he was raised by the Catholic faith
Divided he is by his faith and destiny

To defy the laws of science
Is desirable
To let Nature take its course of evolution
Is unthinkable

Sworn by the oath of his name
He carries out the work of the great ones
Though torn apart by his faith
He hesitates and waits
For the Eagle.

Friendships

Hey friend, how long have we been friends?
I don't know. It's been so long. Do you know?

Hey friend, how come we've been friends
For so long and never once had a fight?
I don't know. I guess it's because we get
Along and have a lot in common. What do you think?

Hey friend, how come our friendship has lasted longer than others?
I don't know friend. Maybe it's because we are open and honest about
Everything. I've been honest with you. Have you?

Hey friend, do you think we will ever grow far apart?
I don't know friend. Only time will tell.
Well times change and so does people.

Hey friend, do you think we will change?
I don't know. People go through tough times?

Hey friend, will you be there for me when the going gets rough?
I don't know. But I will always be there when you need to talk.

Hey friend, what does it mean to be a friend?
I don't know. It means a lot of things for different people. What does it mean to
You when I call you a friend?

Hey friend, what are the rules to a friendship?
I don't know. It's up to the individuals to decide that.

Hey friend, how come we never decided on the boundaries?
I don't know. I guess we expect all Friendships to be the same.

Hey friend, don't you think we should talk about the boundaries before we move
On? It's best we do, so there won't be any misunderstandings.

Hey friend, what's your philosophy on Friendships?
I don't think friends last forever.

Hey friend, why is that?
I don't know. Friends come and go; we make new ones.

Hey friend, can friends fall in love?
I don't know. That's a complex answer which should be discussed amongst
Friends. It can work out if both friends are looking for the same thing.

Hey friend, what keeps our friendship going this long?
I don't know. Maybe it's our communication?

WHAT DO YOU THINK?

You Bring Me Joy

What a wonder it is to know
That you alone brought me Joy.
Who could have imagined
That every waking moment with you
Would bring me so much Joy.

Who knew that
Every smile,
Every laughter,
Every twinkle on your face,
Would bring me so much Joy.

Wow,
What a feeling
Had I known of such Joy existed
When I became a mother for the first time.
There is no other gift so precious as love
That can be given to me by my knight and shining armor.

Thank you for being a loving
Husband,
A father,
& a friend.

But above all things,
Thank God for bringing you
A renewed Joy of life
Once again at 50.

On this day of our Lord
The 19th of June 2011
I proudly celebrate
Father's Day with you and Joya.

Fatherhood

I never knew what it is like to have a father.
I never knew what it is like to have a dad.
I never felt the warmth of my father's hug.
I never heard the words, "I love you son" from my father's mouth.
I never had the love of a father and son relationship with my dad.
I never had the father and son talk that I should have had about life.
I never learned about the birds and the bees from my dad.
I never learned to drive a car from my dad.
I never knew what it is like to play catch with my dad.
Nor have I ever gone to a baseball game with my dad.

But

I only knew the wrath of my father's voice.
I only knew the hand shake of my father's hands.
I only had the presence of a father.
I only knew the anger of a black man.
I only knew the pain, sorrow, and violence of my father's hard life.

I choose to be a dad so I can be a better father then my dad was.
I choose to be a father so my son can have a better role model to look up to.

It's ok that I never had, cause
I can be the role model for the sons who never had.
I can be your example of the father you always wanted to have.
In the end, I learned to embrace the things that I did not want to become, so
I learned to be a better dad from the things that I saw.

Ode to Shakespeare
1564 - 1616

As much as I hated you, I've come to love you!
For the legacy you left behind
A protégé was created in your image.

Today I stand proud with your inspiration imbedded within me.
Each time ink completes a new poem
I am reminded that this work of art was not the end result
Of my own creation but of your inspiration.

The years I've rejected you,
Your style
Your techniques,
Your wisdom,
Father, I beg your forgiveness!

Like every child who has done the unthinkable,
I had forsaken your wisdom and teachings
To spread my own wings
In the 21st Century.

Filled with anger and disgust
I ponder like a muse to create the most simplest of poetic melody
That shall forever be à la mode.

In awe, critiques all over the world shall rebel against
All that was loved and remembered by your pen stroke.

Filled with years of such torment by the academia of my own demise,
I became impregnated with the philosophies of the Greek tragedies of love

Such as
The Odyssey,
Macbeth,
Romeo & Juliet,
Sir Gawain & the Green Knight.

In my desperation to reject your very presence in literature
I too have become a Renaissance man.
Thus writing ballets of love and tragedy
I find myself compelled to write such romantic tales
Of the 21st Century.
Nonetheless I have yet to experience.
I am ashamed to ask,
Am I the rightful heir to thee greatest playwright that has ever lived?
Do I dare to compare thee in the same likeness
Or am I simply an imposter
Reincarnated in your image?
Have I become you in the end
To be living poetry through you
Unbeknown to me!

What would have become of me if I never knew of thee?
The thought alone is unbearable to think!

For you have been my mentor in my endless rage.
To erase you from the educated mind which has taught me well
Is unfathomable!

For I have arrived as a poet and I owe it all to Shakespeare.
For I could not resist but to become you in the end!

The Past & The Present

Oh how times has changed
When we can walk in our neighborhoods and feel safe at night.

Oh how times has changed
When I can call you my brothers & sisters
& trust you at the same time.
When I can speak well of my people.

Oh those were the times
When my neighborhood was free from drugs and crime.
Oh those were the good old days!

Oh how times has changed
When my parents could feel safe at night,
When they felt secure in their homes.

I remember the days when I was proud to say
This is my community, the place I grew up in!
This is my home, my family!

Oh how times has changed
When I could expect to live as old as my parents were
Today I have a better chance of out living my children & grand children

Oh God,
What happened to my people, my community, my family, this world?
What does our future hold for us twenty years from now?

May I never live to see that day Lord!

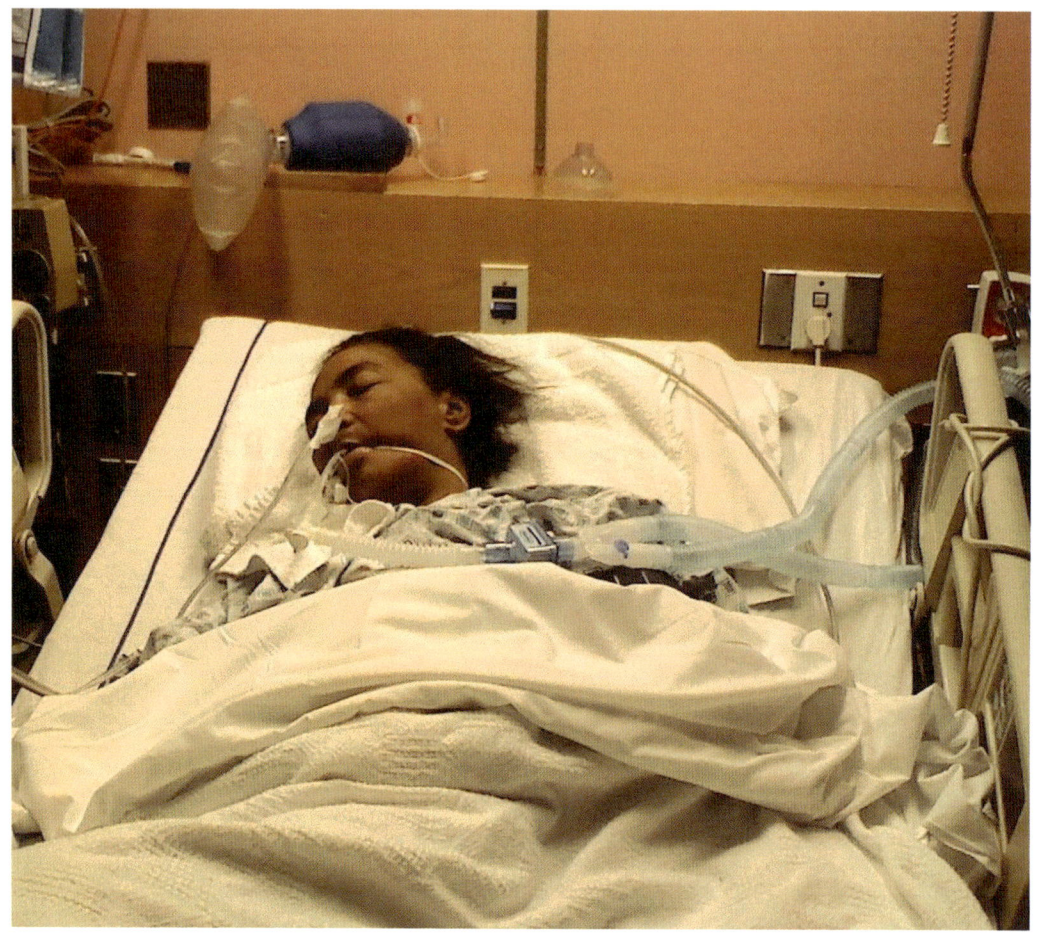

Marva J. Stanton

WINTER 2008
SUMMER 2012

The Silent Fight Within
Dedicated to Marva J. Stanton

Part I

You see, I am the strongest thing living but you couldn't tell from the looks of me. For I am A Warrior Within!

For over 62 yrs. I have defeated the Silent Fight Within
But I was told it couldn't be done. Today, I stand proud before you because I have a fighting spirit that wouldn't give up.

I may not be the strongest, nonetheless the weakest of them all but
I am as determined never to stop fighting The Silent Fight Within.

I was told many lies, although some were true, but many were left at the doorsteps of adolescence. A hospital bed shall forever be my home. Never shall I see my teenage years is what I was told. Only to be a short memory as time stands still for a second to those who breathed life into me. Never shall I conceive a child yet alone live to tell the tales of my labor pains! Nor shall I ever see the glimpse of what's life after birth.

A woman I have become while time stood still for those who stare in disbelief. For once again I have defied the laws of science as I've beaten the odds against my very existence.

You see, I have lived past my time. So to my only son I love, my only wish for you is that of a pure blooded child. For I am a child of God's creation and I have seen the beginning and the end, yet I am on borrowed time.

So listen carefully, but listen good. Child, life is too short and precious, educate yourself today for tomorrow may never come. For my life had meaning for those who lost hope. To see this day is God's will not mine. For I stand before you today so you will never forget the face that has stood the fight, The Silent Fight Within.

You see, Sickle Cell is my enemy. It doesn't have to be yours. Get tested today!
For the life you save may not even be yours, but rather, a grandchild who deserves to be free from all pain and suffering.

So one day, a cure can say,
I went to grandma's to play.

Marva J. Stanton
On her best days

A Warrior Within
Sixty-Three Rounds
Part II

From the looks in your eyes
You could not see my Scarlet Letter "S"

But it is tucked away deep within the scars that run through my veins.

For I am A Warrior Within

It is not a façade that you see me standing here before you.

For I am the strongest thing living today.

Although I bear my Scarlet Letter "S" proudly,

You couldn't tell that I have been through a war,

Yet alone even seen one from the looks of me.

For I am A Warrior Within

I may have never thrown a grenade, held a riffle, nor lost any limbs on the battlefield

But I have been in the ring like a Rocky Balboa part VI.

I have been hit by many punches but my bruises are not visible.

Liver and kidney failure

Seizures

&

Blood transfusions.

I have been knocked out at least three times

4/29/1968

12/23/2006

3/21/2008

Just to name a few.

I am not ashamed

For these were the odds against me

But my coaches' corner has seen me down and out for the count before.

But they all know me too well by now.

It's another grand stand, my claim to fame you see.

It's just another fake out by the grace of God that I stand before you.

There is nothing else that can be said. For I am a child of God's creation,

A Warrior Within!

Coaches Corner

Dr. Ronald Margolin

Dr. Sheldon Lockman

Dr. Darren M. Evanchuk

Assistant Coaches - Nurses

Irene Econonos, RN

Terry Lambert, RN

Elaine Adams, RN

Judy Casale, RN

Thank you,

Marva Jeanette Stanton

Brother Man

Yo, Yo Brother Man can I stop you for a minute?

Yes you, my brotha with the headphones on.

Can you spare a second or two, to rap a minute?

I see you walking down that hill

Every day with that swagger on.

Swaying from side to side.

If I did not know any better I could have sworn

You were Cool Mo Dee

Pimping it like it is easy.

You are one cool cat

All hyped and psyched

To go make that dollar bill.

I've been in your grille

Everyday checking you out

All bright and early you rise

To go make that chedda from the man.

Each time I see you

I say to myself,

Here comes Brother Man heading down the street

Ready to go chase that dollar bill again.

Ain't nothing gonna stop him!

Early to rise

He makes sure he gets to work on time

To make that bread.

Brother Man ain't no fool

Hanging around the street corner,

Eight hours a day smoking a joint

Like them other thugs

Wasting away his life

With a 6 pack at his side,

Being a menace to society.

No, that sure ain't Brother Man

He's a different cat

From another mother.

So Brother Man,

What is the secret to your joy and happiness?

"I'm alive and I've got God in my heart and in my soul."

And off he goes
To make that chedda.

Part IV

Author's Notes

The Story Behind the Poem

Author's Notes:

I want to take this time to thank you for having shared a part of my life's work. I having been writing poetry since I was in high school. I hoped you enjoyed each poem but most importantly I wanted to connect with you as a reader. This section of the book is to start a dialogue online. Once you visit Poetic Imagery In Motion online, you can register as a member and share with me your thoughts on each poem you've read. There will be a comment page for each poem in the book. I really want to know what came to your mind as you read each poem, was there an emotional connection to your life, did you see yourself, or loved ones in the poems you read? You can access the site directly at http://poeticimageryinmotion.com or email me at info@poeticimageryinmotion.com to share your thoughts with me.

I know my method of writing poetry maybe unorthodox. To some it goes against the tradition of how poets are published or recognized as established poets but nonetheless this was how I wanted to express myself to the world. I love being different. I believe we all have a unique God given ability. My book of poems is an extension of that gift. It may be hard for a lot of men especially black men of all things to be able to express himself emotionally but it has never been a problem for me. Nor does it have to mean that I am gay or on the down low. All it means is that God gave me a gift and I am here to share it with you all today.

Each poem written is in fact a page from my heart and the life that I have lived - filled with love and wisdom. I was born out of love and want to leave this world sharing with you a piece of that love every day. That is my gift to you.

In closing, I believe each poem written has a story behind it. I also believe that each poem written has a life of its own that can be expressed visually. This book of poems is only the first step in bringing that to life. Hence each poem is intended to bring out a visual imagery that can come alive in your mind. It is my hope that you will one day enjoy the third phase of all my poems as I bring poetry to life via animation.

For now here is the insight to my thoughts and reason for why I wrote:

"Seeking Soulmate"

When I look back and think about this poem, I always want to laugh for some reason. And that reason is probably because I never believed in online dating until I tried it myself many years later after I had already written this poem. Back in my 20s I was very conservative so the idea of finding someone in a personal ad back in the late 90s was considered a sign of desperation. No one knew the words online dating. If anything you might be thought of as a pervert for picking up women online. Today it is one of the fastest means of finding your mate.

When you analyze this poem, there are two things that I did that I don't recall having done in any of my past poems. I made it humorous and I actually rhymed throughout the whole poem. And like I have said before, that is not something that I do often. Writing about humor is rare for me let alone to write what I would call a love poem that contains any humor.

So it is clearly obvious that I am making fun of myself throughout the poem. Just to think of someone like myself a few years ago putting out an ad sounded weird. And if you look how I place the ad it is exactly how a conservative person who has never done this before would type it. It read like a typical resume. I stated all my attributes without any personality to go with it. As if I was looking more for a job than a girlfriend. What I also find funny about this poem is that I could never picture myself sitting there on Sundays, reading the paper and sipping on coffee as I search in the personals. It's just not something that I would do. And as reality sets in, my old school beliefs kicked in towards the end and decides the only way I am going to find a mate is to go out there and search for her myself.

"The Heavens Above"

I would have to consider *The Heavens Above* my second love poem ever but really my first love. This was one of those poems that came unexpectedly one night as I was taking a drive over to UMass Boston. A little background about me. I went to UMass Amherst to study astronomy. Unfortunately that did not pan out due to life circumstances. Nevertheless astronomy has always been a part of me. Therefore star gazing is a norm for me until that night.

For those who live in the country side can appreciate a beautiful night sky on a regular basis. As a dweller in the city, I would be lucky to see one. So that night was the first time ever that I really got to see the night sky like never before. It was so amazing that I was drawn back. I felt like I was in a spaceship and someone opened the cargo bay doors and was forcing me out to walk in space. That is how clear the sky was that night. I have to say that I was honestly scared and taken back of what I saw that night but at the same time infatuated with the stars.

In the poem, I took the "Heavens" and personalized it to have a deeper yet significant meaning to me. I wanted the poem to describe the perfect encounter I hope to face when I find that special someone I have been searching for all my life. The stars represented to me a mystery, like myself, waiting to be discovered by someone else once you are in that relationship. The mystery that I speak of is the unquenched potential that we see in that person but has not yet been fulfilled. When I look at a shiny star by itself, I see the loneliness that is within. It leaves me to wonder how wonderful would several stars look together instead of it being the only bright star radiating in the night sky.

If you really think about it, it doesn't look the same just like it is our human nature to seek out a mate if not a soul mate for life. Like the stars, finding a partner brings out the best in you. Likewise each star within the night sky is meant to be as one whole completing the bond that unites them all.

When you think about the third stanza, "being put in a daze" and "the description of its beauty" you are really experiencing true love and happiness. The wishing to touch the night sky is symbolic of the unknown that we all fear. So taking the normal precautions of slowly recognizing the joy that goes with being in love for the first time is always unfamiliar territory. The precaution is our way of making sure that what we are seeing and feeling is real.

In closing our first relationship may never be our last one especially when we are young and in love. Hence The Heavens Above suggest that, when we are fearful of entering into a new relationship because we may have been heart broken before, just look at the stars above and those moments of happiness will come back to you.

"Have You Ever"

You know something; I actually walked away from writing poetry for a good four to six years as I pursued other business ventures after college. I really did not know if I still had what it takes to write the way that I use to write. I wondered if I really still had that passion in me the way I wrote love poems, etc. When you go for a long time not doing what you love, you will always come to question whether it was a gift or a craft that you got so use to that you had mastered it. But until it comes back to you naturally that you realize that it was a God given talent and not just something that you were good at at one point in time.

Well I found out in an unlikely place while driving back from Brockton, MA one evening. I was heading home after a meeting with a business associate of mine. I knew she had interest in me but I kept my distance for a good year or so with no intention of pursuing a relationship with her. However things came out in the open about how she felt about me. It seemed she had misconstrued my desire to help her succeed in her business with intentions of pursuing a long term relationship with her because I took the time to listen to her concerns and knew of her struggles. So I was really taken back by her infatuation with me. So much so that I asked myself the question on the way back to Boston if it was possible for someone to have such strong feelings for another person without ever being in a relationship with that person after all. Could we fall in love by simply being in the presence of someone else, by talking to that person, or even just sharing some common idealisms or goals?

I was never certain during my inexperienced love life if such a love that is an infatuation with someone could ever be real but I learned through this poem that it can. I have heard of others using such words but denied it until it happened to me. Until I realized that I have gone through those same emotions as well but did not know that I was only infatuated with that person. It may not be as strong as others may have gone through those same emotions but I realized I have had desires for someone who never knew that I existed or had any interest in them. I just never knew what to call such feelings when I was young.

So I wrote *Have You Ever* with the intent to understand human emotions. How certain things can bring us back to fond memories. I used a lot of my personal experiences in this poem from past relationships to help me recall my infatuations. You can even find traces of pass poems within this poem. I have even added forbidden relationships that we are all too familiar with from our past to relate to all sexes. And that is in part why I put man or woman in parenthesis so you can interchange the sexes base on your sexual preference. After having written this poem, I wanted to make sure that I did not leave anyone out. I know that we all have gone through these roller coasters of love and happiness without the fear of embarrassment or being ridiculed. I wanted this poem to be right for everyone to enjoy without feeling homophobic or a lesbian.

Reading Have you Ever requires that you use your senses to enjoy the imagery that is being portrayed throughout the poem. Whether it is a past lover or a current one, we can all remember how that person smell, taste, or even felt to you in your arms. I took it even a step further and added a line that talks about the moment of conception. I know that there are some women out there that can recall that passionate night when they conceived like clockwork. While some women can forget when they stopped having their period and later found out that they got pregnant, others can instantly remember the day as if it was yesterday. And that is the kind of love making that I am describing throughout the poem. That one person that makes it worth wild to fall in love each and every time.

I have done something different in this poem as well. With each stanza you have to start off repeating the title of the poem. If you have never heard me read it out load, it just may not make sense to you the first time that you read it. Some of you may have to go back and reread it after learning this fact.

"Lady in the Shadow"

I have to say that I have been working on this poem for over ten years. Most of those ten years I spent glancing at it-not knowing what I was going to do with it. It was a fairy tale love story that was in my head for all these years. I was truly stuck for words and did not know in which direction I wanted to go with this poem. Everything changed after I spoke to someone that reminded me about it in directly. Of course it would be fitting that I got inspired to finish this poem overlooking the pier as the time was approaching midnight. Here I was on my cellphone's notepad finishing up the concept behind the *Lady in the Shadow*.

In order to make the vision that I had for this poem work, I had to scrub my traditional love story and come up with a factitious one. I created in my mind a love triangle that could explain this married man's dilemma.

The truth behind this poem is that this man has been hunted in his dreams by this woman in the shadow all of his life. He has fantasized about her since he was a pre-teen but has never been able to see her face. In all of his dreams, he could not see her face or hear her voice. All he knew was the touch of her body, the taste of her lips, and the smell of her fragrance.

The woman in the shadow as it turns out was really never his wife to begin with even though he thought that one day, she was the woman he would marry and have a child with as an adult. In hindsight it is until after he had a child by this woman that he realizes in his dreams that she was never his wife. In actuality it was his mistress that he had an unwed child with. He cries because he is at a loss for words as he has come to love this woman in the shadow for so long that he believed was indeed his wife that he was making passionate love to. Unfortunately he was in fact torn between his fantasy and reality.

The reason why he could never see her face is because he was cheating on his wife and she was always hiding in the darkness of night. So he spends his whole life waiting to meet this woman in real life. So for every woman that passes by him springs off this arousing smell from his dreams of her. At each glance, he ponders the question, are you the Lady in the Shadow? In the end, he never finds out who this woman was in the shadow. So he is always left to wonder who could it be waiting in the shadows.

"Love Potion #8"

Ok maybe I had one more humorous poem in me after all. But this poem really takes the cake as they say. I cannot recall exactly when I wrote this poem but it probably was some kind of homework assignment in school. You can say that this poem is really for the crazy side of love that we sometimes find ourselves in. And I am not talking about infatuations. This is the deep end when you start getting desperate for your man to come back or win his heart kind of crazy.

Some of us may not want to admit it but instead of finding a new partner, we try to fix up the one we have because we tell ourselves all he or she needs is a little fixing. So imagine if we could put a spell on them, the five steps are what would come to mind. Each with its own ingredients and recipe to cure the five common complaints/problems, in this case, about men and their inability to commit to a relationship.

When you read the *Love Potion* being put together, this love doctor sounds more like a witch doctor instead. There is almost a sigh of relief that you can only find this kind of Love Potion in Mama's kitchen. But in comparison the poem is really making a mockery of the border line psychotic things that people tend to do themselves but cannot see the difference. How can this so call love doctor not see the vivid description of holding someone's heart in their hands as not being disturbing. Likewise we sometimes find ourselves sharing things like I slashed his tires, I burnt his clothes, or trash his CD collections with our so call support group for failed relationships. Never seeing how crazy we look for someone that really was never worth your time in the end. At times we find ourselves with bitter friends who encourage you to behave like that.

Having read the disclaimer at the end of the poem, one must think about the title as well. If there is a Love Potion #8, what in the world would the first seven potions look like? Could you imagine what else this love doctor has in her kitchen cabinets? Here's a clue, think about all of the crazy relationships you have gone through just to find that someone special and you can fill in the blanks.

"Lost Love"

This poem was originally an E-Card email that I had sent out to an ex-girlfriend of mine. We had stayed as friends over the years but would once in a while exchange E-Cards on birthdays and Valentine's Day. I had liked what I wrote so much that I decided to turn it to a poem and call it *Lost Love* as a reminder for those who have loved dearly.

We never forget our first love but more importantly we never forget that person who made us feel special inside. These are the kind of relationships we never forget growing up as adults. Sometimes we yearn to rekindle those moments in time. For whatever reason we all know that old relationship will never work out again but we force ourselves to dwell in it as long as we could hold on to them. At some point we all have to let go and say goodbye but there is a part of us that still holds on to that memory. From time to time we find ourselves wondering of the possibilities. The potential of that relationship had it lasted.

In the end, we all hope that they will mature in time to see their errors in judgment of the love they had lost. Hoping that at some point in their life, they will call you back to tell you that you were in fact the best thing that ever happened to them.

We all have someone that we are waiting for. And sometimes someone else is waiting on us. Therefore what are you waiting for, make that phone call, sent out that email, Search for that Lost Love and tell them… "You were the best thing that happened to me!"
Even though it may take eternity, I am still waiting on you.

"Ode to an Apple"

Wow, what can I say? That is the most seductive visual poem that I ever wrote. It was the first of its kind. This poem is the kind of poem that you cannot just read to anyone. It will just make you blush and leave you speechless. I always give my disclaimer up front so no one gets offended in case they were not expecting that. Like I tell all my female friends when I read this poem to them, you will never look at an apple the same. You probably never thought that one could describe an apple like that.

I think if you had to describe a woman's body part in a sexual way, the apple would suit you fine without getting too graphic. And that is what I wanted to convey in this poem. I wanted it to be sensual but yet clean without being too vulgar. The visual depiction of the apple left plenty of room for your mind to wonder if anything else it fills in the blinks.

The poem itself was probably a college assignment given to me a few years ago. Years later I can hardly recall how I came about to really write this poem but most likely it was what I had to work with. My professor probably gave me an apple and told me to write about it. So I wrote about what I knew best and what I envisioned when I looked deep into that apple. Maybe if you look at it again from my viewpoint you will see the same thing.

"When We First Made Love"

Have you ever wondered what the experience would be like from a man's perspective when you first make love to him? This poem kind of describes the emotions that this young man is experiencing after having intercourse with his lover for the first time. Of course the young man is impressionable and is in love with this woman. So every possible touch or connection he had experienced he is sharing it with you. Even what he believed would happen when he first touch her he has already imagined the experience in his mind.

It is clearly obvious that this person is a virgin and has remained pure throughout this time until he found the love of his life. It is without a doubt to say that this man is definitely in touch with his feminine side. Yet he is still a passionate man that is not afraid to express his feelings towards her. The emotion is unbearable that he cries at the end.

"There is No One Else Like You"

I originally wrote this poem for my girlfriend at the time. I would later use the first half of this very poem to propose to her. The poem itself is more like two poems in one. It starts off as a regular passionate poem but later turns into a primate or barbaric type of poem. And the reason I did that was to capture a man's point of view when seeking out his mate. The way we think of our mate when we are courting or seeing her for the first time is like that wild animal in the jungle. All that I describe is no different from what a cave man would see and experience as he approaches the opposite sex today. In the 21st century, the process really does not seem that much different to man. The first sight of a beautiful woman is over taken by our primal instincts to attack and claim her as our own. If anything the poem reminds you of the process of natural selection.

What I did different was put a black woman's twist into the mix. Making her stronger than ever before. Giving her the recognition for all that she had endured throughout history. I illustrated every characteristic of a black woman and made her stronger so that brothers would not confuse what would be perceived as weak traits from strength. I guess my message is that a woman can be anything and everything besides the prize of a man's heart.

"Your Eyes Told Me"

Have you ever looked deep into the soul of a man or a woman from simply looking at their eyes? Within the glow you can see their soul and determine if they were a good person or not? Well I believe that I have the gift to see that in people. Most importantly when it comes to relationships we all can tell, especially if you are a woman, how genuine is your man when he says he loves you or when he is making love to you. There is something magical that happens in the eyes as if they are glowing. It is one of the most vulnerable parts to our hearts. It is at this point in your relationship that it becomes most intimate. I believe it is at this point that you are truly bonding with that person in your life.

I have shared many moments where I would look deep into a woman's heart and see that glow that I speak of but there are only few that share the spark that tells you whether he or she is the one you want to spend your whole life with. And that is what we are really searching for when we look deep at the eyes of our mate. All the insecurities, desires, passion, aspirations that we feel towards that person is illuminated at that moment. The worries go away. It brings us a sense of peace and tranquility that we can confide our deepest secrets to that one person.

I myself used this poem to express to my girlfriend how I felt about her. I later on rewrote the ending to fit appropriately the day that I asked her to marry me. It is one of my proudest moments in my life that I share with you and hope you too will use this poem one day when you are ready to propose to your significant other.

"Thank You Lord"

When I was in college, I befriended someone who found out that I write poetry. One summer she asked me to write a poem for her. She was a very religious person at the time that I met her in college that I reflected on her spiritual life and wrote a poem that I thought she would appreciate. *Thank You Lord* was my very first spiritual poem that I had ever written; it was my first request by anyone at the time, and the only poem that I wrote in this format thus far. I wanted the poem to have a churchy hymn psalm look to it and that was my thinking behind the format of this poem.

As it is customary when people ask me to write them a poem, I start to freak out in my head because the way that I write is from a personal standpoint that is very intimate with knowing the person who is making the request. Nevertheless I always worry that I will not be able to do a good job but somehow the words always seem to pour out of me on paper when I put my mind to it. And that was the same thing that happened with this poem.

With the intention of writing a religious poem for my friend, I began to think about the kinds of welcoming messages that we see at people's houses. Like the doormats may have some kind words as you enter someone's home. Being that I come from a Catholic upbringing, I automatically reflected on the nice prayer plaques that I use to see at people's houses.

After having seen the effort that I put in that poem and how prayerful it was, I really envision this poem being at everyone's house. I myself saw it hanging at my mother's house for visitors to see it. I just thought it was such a powerful prayer poem that I was really impressed with my own God given talent. The last few stanzas were in acknowledgement to God that I was not going to take the talent that he gave me lightly. Therefore I did not want to take anything that was given to me for granted.

"The Four Seasons"

In 2011 I joined a poetry club called Lyric Poetry that was trying to revive itself for the umpteenth time. It was my first time hearing about it and I wanted to check it out. One of my assignments was to write a poem inspired by another poet. One of the poets that I read from the anthology given to me was Gwendolyn Brooks', "A Sunset of the City." The poem made me think about *The Four Seasons* of Mother Nature. It made me reflect on what each season symbolize to us from a spiritual yet nurturing level. I was also introduced for the first time to a new format called Haiku. I was impressed when I first learned about it but never thought I could write one. In writing The Four Seasons, I kept that format in mind. This was my best attempt at doing a Haiku poem.

When it comes to writing poetry, I never like restricting myself to a certain format, stanza, etc. I usually prefer to express my thoughts on paper first than attempt to put some kind of poetic form to the poem afterwards. It's just like rhyming. I can never do it. It was not a gift that came naturally. Traditionally I don't write short poems. This as you can see is probably the best that may ever come out of me in less than half a page. I recall reading such poems in college and I would really ask myself if these so called "well known" poets were even for real. How could you call that poetic? That was my usual thought process when I see poetry like that. Well to be frank with you, I never considered those types of writings to be serious work. Being able to express oneself was something that I regard as valuable. Therefore three or four short phrases could never be considered artistic in my eyes. Boy was I wrong. And that is why poetry like art is always left to the imagination to define and interpret what is artistic or poetic.

"That's True Love"

I consider this to be one of my most heartfelt poems each time I read it. I started to write this poem in memory of one of my friends who lost her father. She was very distraught about it. However I wrote the poem from her mother's perspective. She was an elderly woman married since she was a young girl to the same man-her only true love. I wanted to capture that love in this poem by writing a poem that I felt would capture her emotions throughout the grieving process. As I continued to write, I thought about other wives who may have lost a soulmate. The anger, emptiness, or hurt they might have felt over the loss of their partner. I too found myself using my own pain and emotions if I had to lose my wife.

In an attempt to read this poem, one must exhume a lot of anger and tiers filled with rage. That is how I wrote it from beginning to end. Each time I read it, I visualized the anger and the pain so much that I want to cry. The poem itself is a love story that captures you in the moment as the funeral proceeds. Having gone through my share of funerals I have seen all types of emotions being expressed and I used that to emulate a widow's pain. A few of the lines that I used in the poem is from what I have heard stated to a grieving widow over the years.

I ended the poem with the expectation that she will join him very soon because I have seen such love as deep as that friend wither till they too are dead because of such emptiness. I have always believed that there is such a love connection so strong that one cannot do without the other for long. And the one remaining will eventually find themselves back with their mate in due time. That in essence is always *True Love*.

"Season's Greetings"

December 2009 was a very interesting year for my new wife and I. It was the first time that we celebrated Christmas without our kids. They had become an integral part in my life. It just was not the same without them. Nonetheless we went through the motions.

I also had started a new chapter in my life. I got involved in October of that year in my church's poetry ministry called, Lyric Ministry. With the rules solely focus on Christian style poetry only was something that I was not all too sure of at first but I stayed to see what will happen and most importantly what would come of it. I figured if anything I can tap into that spiritual side of me some more and write some great poems if anything else. So this poem was actually my first assignment. To write up to a 30 line poem about advent, being in the Christmas, New Year spirit. I myself was not really sure what I was going to write.

Eventually I began to get inspirited just as the week of Christmas came. I thought of several ideas of what I wanted to write but was not definite on any one of them. This is when I started getting these text messages from family and friends during Christmas eve and Christmas day. I started to pay attention to what was written. They were all similar phrases and sayings that we tend to send to all of our friends and families during the season. So I began to save a few lines from each text message. The ones that I selected were sweet and comforting words that were truly expressive of the atmosphere of Christmas and a new year. I too began to feel that atmosphere of love, wishful thinking, of God, and being more reflective on our lives this time of year.

Fortunately a friend of mine whom I befriended a few short months prior from work sent me an Obama campaign email wishing me *Season's Greetings*. It was a very effective email that actually displayed my name in the message. Similar to the one that was being spread out through the internet via email to go out and vote for Obama during the election of 2008. After having watched that video clip, I was really inspired by the various diverse cultural phrases wishing someone a Merry Christmas or Happy New Year within their respective tongue or religious affiliation. Hence leading me to create this very poem and using that email's subject line.

In the process of formatting the poem, I started playing with the stanzas. To my surprise, the words formed a tree like symbolic of life. I was really impressed by it and also unaware of this other fact as well. As I checked the stanza count, it actually added up to the required 30 lines unbeknown to me. So from the distance looking at this poem, you can actually see this symbolic tree form taking place within each stanza. In closing, after I was all done with the poem, unconsciously, I created everything that I wanted to accomplish with the poem without really thinking too much about it. It just came to life naturally. So you never know where inspiration will come from.

"This Christmas 2007"

I would have to say that 2007 was the highlight of my life. Although things were not perfect, I felt that I was on my way. I was on a high for life. I finally saw hope for me and a glimpse of the promise God has for me. This poem was in praise of God's doing. For me it was the best Christmas ever. It was the year that I proposed to my girlfriend. It was the year that I found my better half.

The notion of being married one day has always been a very important part of my journey through life. Knowing that I had finally found the person God intended for me to be with was a blessing. I inherited two beautiful daughters in the process. Things were getting better financially. All was good. The Christmas atmosphere was really blossoming around my life. I felt very blessed. I have never looked forward to a new year like I did for 2008. It felt like a cloud of uncertainty was being lifted off my life. As it is stated in the Bible, seven symbolizes the order of completion. Therefore eight must be the number for new beginnings.

It truly felt like a new beginning was on the rise. Therefore I began thinking of *This Christmas* as a title for this poem while I was watching a movie at the theatre, namely enough it was called, "This Christmas." It was not until I attended service that Sunday morning did I feel the Holy Spirit talking to me through the sermon that was given at church. The message was all empowering. I was uplifted, triumphant, full of hope, and clarity. I felt a big burden was lifted off my shoulder. I believed in the Word that my breakthrough was near. For the first time in my life, I felt like I was free. Free from the stress of life, from the day to day struggle of trying to make ends meet, and free from the worldly possessions that keeps us down. As you can tell from this prayer, I was truly in the whelm of receiving God's blessings. That Sunday I felt the shackles were removed as I thought of Dr. King's struggle to set us free. I hoped you were empowered through this poem to seek out your freedom from whatever that keeps you back from reaching the destiny that God has planned for you.

Just a quick note, in the last stanza I reference the words, "I wise" for I am free! The misspelling is done deliberately because that is the title of another poem that I am referencing to. It is a poem that I am still working on and will probably come out in the next volume of poems. The words reflect that I have not only risen from the mess I was in but that I have gained wisdom through the process. I have always believed that it is wisdom that carries us forward. And I am always learning from my mistakes as well as the mistakes of others. Hence you should not just rise from your obstacles in life, you should wise up with a greater sense of clarity as you move forward.

"The Last Sunset:
An Ode to Lyon Heart"

We all know what it means to lose a love one. Tears, pain, sorrow, anger, or sympathy are words that may describe how a person should feel after losing someone they knew. For me that was not the case. It was the feeling of emptiness because I really did not know my uncle since he was just a stranger to me. Like a family friend who came to visit once in a while was how I saw my uncle. A naval doctor who lived most of my childhood in California was all that I knew of him. A picture frame on the wall was how I attached the name to the face.

When he came back home for good, it was not a joyous occasion for my family. He had just discovered that he had gotten the AIDS virus from a blood transfusion. Until the late 80s no one tested blood transfusions for diseases, infections, yet alone AIDS. So it was a shock to our family. One that needed to be kept silent because of the ignorance that came with having

AIDS in the family. Today many of us are educated on the origin of AIDS and how it is passed on. At the time, being Haitian and having AIDS was considered to be one in the same.

At his funeral I did not know how to relate to him, feel emotionally, or act around the people that loved him most. So I did what I knew best. I started thinking of this poem. I wrote it in my head while I was observing those that were in moaning.

When I began thinking about *The Last Sunset*, I wanted to portray him as a hero, a family man, a well decorated Naval officer, a leader amongst his peers, and last but not least a warrior. I saw within him a lion who was king of his jungle. And that was how I wanted to remember my uncle from a child's point of view.

So this poem is dedicated to Lyonel Frederique and all those who have died from the virus. This was my way of communicating to him that I loved him, had the highest respect for him during the time that I got to spend with him, and that I acknowledged his death.

May the heart of the Lyon rest forever.

"Am I the One?"

I have done a lot of soul searching over my life time and this was the most painful one of them all. You could even say that I was in a spiritual warfare with God and his plans for my life. I was fighting complacency and contentment versus what I knew God had in store for my life. Everything changed for me when I sat down at church one evening. The choir was singing and this song rang out in my heart as I began to cry. My pastor later preached that evening a powerful sermon entitled, *Am I the One*? And all I could hear was God talking to me. And he was asking me whether or not I believed in myself that I was chosen to change the world, change my life, and make a difference. That sermon spoke to me and my desire to be great to be an entrepreneur. To be that man that God had called me out to be at birth. To be that leader he saw in me. I had to believe it. And this poem in itself is a prayer to God asking myself that very question, Am I the One?

A year later, I would begin to write one of the most powerful books ever written about business. And in the process I have kept this poem that I started in 2008 in the back of my mind for this very book that would change my life around. I felt it was necessary to include this poem in there. So I rewrote it to fit the book, *Why Entrepreneurship*. It is my first novel on business.

I believe there are many of us in the religious community who struggle with the notion of whether God has a plan for us. We tend to ponder at that question for years before we find the thing that we have been searching for or hearing the call for. As I stated in *Why Entrepreneurship*, I believe that God called all of us to be great at birth but few heard the calling while others simply ignored it and went about their business. Meanwhile there are hundreds more that are searching for an answer. That answer is hidden within the very question that is asked of us. Are we worthy to understand the plan that God has for each one of us? It is my hope that this problem will lead you to the right path.

Although the original ideas and notes for this poem were started in 2008, I have added a few lines here and there over the years. But it was not until August of 2012 that I finally completed this poem. However my faith has since grown stronger and I have more to contribute to this poem from a new understanding of my purpose in life.

Usually when I write, I do not think of a stanza format. It just comes to me as I began to structure each poem. Nonetheless I found it intriguing to share some interesting facts about this particular poem. When I looked back at some of the lines that I wrote, I notice 33 as a significant number from a biblical stand point. Jesus was 33 when he began his journey. At this point in my life, I too was 33 years of age. Everything sort of made sense in hindsight.

I also wrote this poem with a 5 and 7 line stanza in mind unbeknown to me at first. Once I noticed what was happening, I flowed with its symbolism. Five represented the work week. Doing the grind five days a week is normal. For most of us in corporate America, that is a great schedule. For those who have the entrepreneurial spirit like me, it is not enough. Seven is referred to throughout the poem. Seven days of the week representing the completion of a cycle. God created the Earth in seven days - a new beginning in the religious world. The first seven years of the new millennium was concluded by 2008, a new beginning.

When you read the last line, it is a single stanza. Likewise you will notice that each time God is recognized or begins to speak, the poem starts a fresh line to represent the beginning of something new. Even the conclusion of the poem ("Lord, if it is your will") when I seem to start to understand God's path for me, that line is singular. I did it to symbolize that I too was walking in clarity and starting new in the image of God.

"Unborn Love"

I wrote this poem while I was still in the waiting room as my wife was recovering from the loss of another baby. We were so sure this time it would be ok. We prayed each night and held each other when we thought about the worst case scenario as she began to bleed. This was our second and longest miscarriage. I had so much high hopes that this pregnancy was the one. I did not know what to do but reflect on the situation in my head and put words on paper that cried out for my pain.

I almost did not know how to feel because I was the man that had to play the supporting role because this in fact was a time to be there for your partner. But what about me? I asked myself that question throughout the poem. Who was going to console me and what I was going through? And I realized that I did not have anyone but a pamphlet on my lap. As I look back upon that day, I pray that you may never have to grow through this pain that we had to endure. Nevertheless for those men who have lost an *Unborn Love* like I have, may this poem bring you the comfort and peace that you need for closure.

"Knocking on Heavens' Door"

On April 30th 2010, I lost a member of my family. I asked that I give the eulogy for the funeral. Janina was not someone that you can say that I was close to but she was indeed a very important member of our family. Prior to her death, I attended a funeral service just two weeks before for Jackie Lee Brown better known as Mommy's Big Head who had passed away from Non-Hodgkin Lymphoma. I did not know the man but only his mother through my wife. But his death and ceremony was still on my mind. He was only forty-four years old and my great aunt was actually ninety-two. Now during the same time frame, I have been writing my first book, *Why Entrepreneurship – What is IT all about?* I spent a lot of time writing about fulfilling our purpose in life and living a life filled with significance. So I had a lot to reflect on the subject before writing this poem.

However writing a poem was the furthest thing from my mind until the funeral was over. It was the first time that I actually stayed long after the refreshments were served at our family's house. Usually I never like to stick around after the funeral. Watching people laughing and drinking after having buried a loved one always bothered me. So I am usually the first one to leave right after. But this time around, I had some time to kill and I wanted to do some relaxing and take in the fresh air. I wanted to enjoy the peace and quiet of the hot spring day. So I sat there and closed my eyes and began enjoying the breeze of fresh air. It was a beautiful moment. In the background, I could hear the laughter and voices of my family members who were in town. My sister was there, cousins, and other friends and family. As I began to day dream, my thoughts went back to the previous day as I was speaking to my uncle about us growing apart as we get older. We were such a tight big family but with age we began to drift apart. All of those thoughts were in my head as I laid there outside the patio that day. Then it dawned on me that I should actually write a general poem about people losing family and loved ones. This poem was not intended for a specific person or family member. I wrote it with everyone in mind. It was written so that everyone would think about their life. Apart from when we experience the loss of a loved one, that is usually the only time that people reflect on the big question of their significance in their lives. The title was taken from the last paragraph that I wrote in my eulogy to her, "Wherever you are now in heaven's door." After hearing the phrase several times, I fell in love with the title. I thought that it would serve as a great title to a poem. Soon after, I envisioned someone knocking in heaven as I laid there quietly enjoying the sun in the shade. It became the theme for the poem.

It is good trivia to know that I wrote this poem all from my cell phone. Ever since I began writing half of my book on my phone, I have used it as my favorite note pad when thoughts or ideas come to mind. Usually I save my notes but this time, the whole poem was finished on my cell phone. When I went through editing it, I added a few lines here and there but it dawned on me that it felt complete when I restructured the poem. So I ended up leaving it as it was.

I did not structure the stanzas like I usually do with my poems. I wanted to limit as little periods as possible because I wanted to reflect what infinity fills like throughout the poem. I wanted the poem to flow and not fill restricted.

"- My Eulogy -
Please Read in My Absence"

I truly love the title of the poem. It is as if I don't fear death or even recognize that I have passed on. Like I am just giving someone a note or a message to give in my absence and I will be back another time. Well that is exactly how I feel about dying. Your body is physically gone but your presence is still here on Earth. Meaning the impact that you have made in the world would be an ever lasting legacy in the hearts of those you've left your foot print with.

For most people dying is a grim thought that we tend not to want to talk about. For me I have never feared death but believe that I will be prepared the day that I die. I am comfortable with the notion that one day I will leave this Earth like everyone else. Hopefully of natural causes is the way I would like to go. My only concern as the poem suggest is that I have made a big enough impact that everyone that I have known will miss my presence; that I have lived a life of significance.

The inspiration behind this poem was a direct impact of two things that occurred in my life in 2010. The year started out with the first funeral which was normal but by October of the same year that I wrote this poem, my wife and I had gone to at least eleven out of what would become thirteen funerals of friends and family members between the two of us by the end of the year. Needless to say it was more than the sheer amount of deaths and funerals that I have ever experienced in my entire life in one year.

When you go through that many funerals in one year, I think it would have a big impact on anyone especially someone like me who spends a lot of time thinking about the future, reflecting on my life, and observing the world around me. If anything else it should make you think about when will your time be up? What will you accomplish in the time that God gives you? Well it sure did it for me.

That same year as it was coming to a close, my Lyric Poetry club had given me an assignment from an anthology of selected poems that I had to choose from. One of the poems was from Tupac Shakur's, *"In the Event of My Demise."* Up to this point, I have never read anything about Tupac except having heard his music on the radio let alone knew that he was a poet himself. I knew that he could rhyme and rap-that he was a deep brother when it came to his lyrics but I was blown away when I read that poem.

Just from the title of the poem itself was captivating and spiritual because I very well knew of his tragic death. He had foreseen his demise to come. Likewise I was working on my first business book on the topic of purpose and living with a sense of significance. Naturally I could relate to him and so were the words that I inked on paper. Having read his poem, "In the Event of My Demise" I was instantly reminded of this poem that I had been meaning to write for a long time. And that was the start of *My Eulogy*.

I have always been an opinionated person. One who loves to think and express myself intellectually. So why would I let someone else do the speaking for me was my thought process as I wrote this poem. It was as if it was my last will and testament that I was assigning to my wife to read on my behalf. Therefore as the analytical person that I am, it is fitting that even at my funeral I would want to control what was said about me. There are some specific things that I wanted to make sure people knew about the man that will one day lay in that coffin. I have never been the type to take certain things to chance. Having attended so many funerals and heard many eulogies, I have always wondered what my funeral would be like. Who would attend? What would people say about me once I am gone? In business I have been taught that the size of people who attends your funeral is dependent on the weather that day. Being a curious person, I could see myself asking for a grace period before I am ascended just so I can attend my own funeral and see who really mattered in my life. Who would actually show up despite of it all?

Having been a legacy driven man, I wrote the poem as a wish list or a bucket list of things that I had hope to have accomplished before my demise. We all have goals and dreams that we strive to accomplish within the life that was given to us. Many of us never get to fulfill all of our dreams and aspirations. We just do the best we can with the hands that life dealt us. So having taking the time to reflect on my life and the life hear after, this poem said all that I wanted to say about my life and what I had hoped to achieve.

"Who Am I"

I was inspired to write this poem shortly after I had attended the Million Man March in 1995. Throughout my four years at UMass Amherst where I attended college, I was known for studying late nights at the New Africa House in Central. That was my safe haven from all the commotion that is UMass. Each night I was surrounded by African art, artifacts, paintings on the wall, etc. All to remind me of my heritage. One evening I took the time to reflect at all that was around me and I began to write. These three life changing experiences played a large part in how I saw myself as a freshman in college.

 As an individual who was raised Catholic-having gone to Catholic schools all of my life, and then to UMass, it was a culture shock for me to adjust to my new environment-very diverse and definitely different from what I was accustom to. Furthermore I began noticing something different about the African American students that attended UMass.

For some but not all were losing their self-identity. At times when we start something new, we tend to forget who we are as a person and where we came from. For a lot of us coming to UMass, we tend to lose track of our purpose for going there. Instead we find ourselves so caught up in the life that is UMass – the social networks, partying every weekend, and drinking that we forget even our own identity.

In light of all that, I did not want to lose myself, my identity before I leave UMass. So this poem began as a self-evaluation of me and to question *Who Am I* and what I have become over the years and where I wanted to go from here. Along the way, I found myself wanting to proclaim my identity to the world. I wanted to remove society's labels on me. I wanted to be free to express myself but also to identify with those who have lost their own identity. This poem evolved to being the voice for the hopeless. I became the voice for all that is possible in the world. In closing I want you to find your own identity. Not through someone else's vision of you but your own vision of who you are. Life is hard enough for you to lose faith in God's plan for you so always ask yourself, Who Am I.

One last thought, if you are wondering why there is no question mark on the title, it's because I have always known who I am. A child of God is never really lost. The title of the poem was never about me asking the question of myself but of you.

"The Eagle"

Looking back at this poem many years later, I have to believe that the poem, *Who Am I* and the Million Man March played a significant role in the way that I saw myself in the mirror. I was a sophomore in college when I wrote this poem about myself. During my tenure at UMass Amherst, I studied Astronomy and learned of the many great scientists that bore my name. In my eyes, it was an honor to be given such a great name with a lot of high expectations behind it. Over the course of my education, I learned a lot about the various Dimitris that preceded me in my science classes. Fortunately for me, they were all German or Russian names all spelled slightly different from mine, Dimitry with a Y at the end and not an I. It was not up until my mid-thirties that I found someone who actually had the same spelling as me. I take pride in being one of a kind.

Growing up I found myself to be my own self motivator and the type of guy who likes to do things differently than others. I also saw the world different from a scientifically curious open eye perspective you could say.

Earlier on in my childhood I found myself attracted to Eagles and what they stood for. I have always said if I had to be defined by a symbol; it would be that of *The Eagle*. If anything FREEDOM was what I wanted out of life. But as irony prevailed, I was torn by two worlds. One being a scientific world filled with technology and the other a Catholic upbringing. Sometimes I feel torn between the two because of what I was learning in school versus what I knew about God and my faith.

Having been born with a scientific mind, I had to let go of a lot of unexplained ideologies without facts. Nevertheless my religious upbringing would not allow me to let go. So this poem at the time was my illustration of the battle that was going on in my head and in my heart. Two opposites that I dearly love. One does not recognize the other in the real world but yet I found myself right in the middle of it all.

Having read my first volume of poems, you can often find me expressing my love of both. However one had to dominate the other. Today I take great pride in knowing that I can separate the two and know what is God and what is indeed explainable by science. For God is the overseer of my life. And my writings are exemplary of all that I am and nothing less. But at the end of the day, I do leave it all up to God.

"Friendships"

Friendships are one of our sacred bonds we all share with the world. Whether it is one friend or many friends, we all have them. How sacred we value those friendships is what this poem is all about. I am one who values all of my friendships because I choose to have few then many. Others choose to have a lot as a means of comfort while people like me who are loners choose to keep a handful of friends if not less. During the course of my life I have recognized that there are only three types of friendships, the one who is your best friend, the one who you hang out with once in a while, and the one who you are cordial with at work, see at social networking events, or touch base with once in a blue moon.

I believe that every friend in our lives serve a purpose. They are put in place either for a reason or a season of your life. I never understood that until I was in college and lost two good friends of mine at the end of my second semester. This made me question how sacred is our friendships and do we really know what being a friend is all about? Do we value them at all? This poem is meant for all of us to challenge ourselves and ask a lot of the unspoken questions about our friendships with one another.

We have this idea that all friendships will last forever but we forget that a friendship is just like any other relationship we venture into. So as you re-read this poem, call either someone you call a true friend or grab them if they are sitting next to you and look at each other in the eye, listen carefully, and remember to ask these questions of one another later on in life when your friendship reach that shaky point. Later on, if you really care to salvage your broken friendship, then remember the words to this poem.

"I don't think friends last forever" has been one of my philosophies of life. I share that towards the end of this poem. I have to say in retrospect, the true friends that were meant to be in my life have stayed long after the moment has past. Last but not least, the best friends you meet are the ones you should not neglect to consider as a life time partner. I found mine and I am glad she is my friend.

To Friendships….

"You Bring Me Joy"

In 2011 a good friend of mine asked me to write a poem for her. She had just gotten married the year before and had just given birth to her first born daughter named Joya. When I thought about her original request, it was supposed to be a poem for herself. However as I began thinking of her daughter's name Joya, I wanted to do something different that would be a play off on her name alone. Timing was also perfect as father's day was near and so was her husband's birthday. So I decided to write the poem from her perspective to him while giving thanks for their new born baby. This poem was short and to the point while covering all the aspects of their newlywed life together.

When I gave it to her, I made sure that she read it out loud to him. I knew it would be more memorable to him if he heard it from her voice first rather than reading it and seeing that it was a man that wrote it. I knew it would not have the same affect that I had hope would touch him if he knew the voice behind the ink.

"Fatherhood"

I don't think that there are many people who can say they have had a father and son relationship like I did. I lived with my father for a good portion of my life at home but I could not say that I knew the man. The factors that put the rift between us will never change. At this stage of my adult life, I could not say that I really care for it. My father never did anything for my mom. I found myself always doing for her or being her protector if not her son. At times I found myself filling the role of both husband and son.
I can never forget the way I grew up though. Part of me yearning to be a father myself is to have a better relationship with my own son. So one day I could do all the things that I never did with my father.

It just so happened that one morning I woke up early to take my mom to her 5:00 AM bus trip to Pennsylvania thinking about all the things I never got to experience with my dad. In the process of waiting for her to be picked up, I started thinking about these words, "I never had a dad, I never knew what it is like to have a father, etc…" That was the start of *Fatherhood*. I felt compelled to write about being a dad. The poem evolved to being more than just about my dad but about all sons who never had a chance to know their father.

The poem's rhythmic sad melody is supposed to draw the reader in. Making you feel like a kid writing about his family life from the viewpoint of an adult. I also deliberately left the present tense form of "is" in the second to last line of the first stanza to signify that I like all sons also have a choice to correct that. It's never too late. Cause for those who may not know this, I wrote this during the years my dad was alive. For most, the poem would suggest that a kid is writing this poem as an orphan when in fact that is not the case. In all, I wanted to reach out to other kids in my situation and show them that it can and will get better. The loss of not having a father around is very tough to deal with and I wanted to portray to them that I will be that role model for them. I wanted to ensure that they knew they all had a segregate father through this poem. And that they too can change the circumstance of another child's life when they themselves become an adult one day. The memories of emptiness alone should make you never want to allow your own child to experience that kind of loneliness. Fatherhood is a great privilege and not a choice that can be ignored. A father's love is always wanted.

"Ode to Shakespeare"

This poem is a dedication to what he has created in my desire to erase the gift that he gave me in the process. How I became a poet was because I wanted to be different from what Shakespeare tried to create. My purpose for writing poetry was to erase all that was complex about Shakespeare. To rebel against all that was loved by him. Instead I found myself becoming him to a certain extent. I had the intention to just write simple poems that ordinary folks would understand. I was once told that the poems that he wrote were not created for the common man but rather the upper class of society. So my intention was to write poems for the less snotty and uneducated folks that was left out during his era. However as I became a better writer, I realized that I did not want to just write poetry with ease so that everyone would understand it. I found that I really wanted to challenge the intellectual minds of those who read my poems. Therefore like Shakespeare, they should challenge themselves to have a vivid imagination so they would envision in one's mind what I was trying to create. Hence leaving everyone with their own interpretation.

In most of my love poems, you will find that I wrote certain words or say certain things that leave the possibility of a double meaning or interpretation. I guess it is the curiosity and mystery in me that has rubbed off from Shakespeare's work over the years. Nevertheless the poet in me came out without even an inkling of becoming a poet. What started out as one poem has developed to several others that would follow.

But on the contrary, my love for Shakespeare did not start out like that. It took me many years later before I would come to admire and respect the poet and play writer for his ingenious creations. Originally I was introduced to poetry by Mr. Bill Collins who was my high school ESL teacher for many years. It was because of him that I fell in love with a few writers along the way like-Sir Gawain & the Green Knight. This was how I learned about chivalry and how men stood for honor and their words were bond by the shake of a hand. We spent countless months analyzing and dissecting that book. Looking back, I would have to say it was those kinds of writings that made me become the love poet that I am today. The ideals of honor, respect, loyalty, ethics, and trust definitely influenced the way I write about love, spiritual, and spoken words poems.

However when it came to Shakespeare's work, I had a tough time understand much of what he was saying. Nonetheless I did manage to find a few books and plays that he wrote, such as Macbeth and Romeo & Juliet etc. that started to make sense to me- probably because they related to love.

I also learned to build a hatred for other things about Shakespeare's work before I did fall in love with him. Mainly that people would spend centuries trying to understand or write thesis on the man's work. I would ask myself at times if his intention was to be as simple as saying hi but we as intellectuals began to make it turn out to be more complex than what it was intended for. Although we may never know the real reasoning behind some of his works of genius, it still left a mystery to be desired by all who read and tried to understand him. As much as I admired that in Shakespeare, I refuted the notion by starting my own background story on every poem that I wrote so folks would not waste so much time trying to dissect my poems like they did with Shakespeare. Hence is the reason why you are reading this author's note. I believe that every poem written has a story behind it and I wanted to share them with you. I wanted you to understand my vision behind each poem but most importantly I wanted to know what you got out of that poem for yourself. With each poem that I write, my intention is to bring about an emotional connection to the reader. With the emphasis always being on simplicity; I think I have stood by my convictions in writing simplistic poems for the commoner but with a Shakespearean twist to it.

In closing, *Ode to Shakespeare* is a symbolic poem that I began while I was in college. It was the epiphany that I was waiting for to make me embrace poetry as a passion of mind. What I use to think was a bunch of crap that was being forced upon me in school, has turned out to be one of the greatest things that I have come to love and hope to make a success of it as a business. It is my hope that the concept behind the type of formats I choose to express my vision for each poem would be greatly appreciated by William Shakespeare as he was truly a visionary that can never be duplicated. So my work is to bring about the emotions through visual conception and imagery that Shakespeare so triumphantly demonstrated in his work. I hope to one day be as admired as he has been for centuries.

"The Past & The Present"

I came up with the idea for this poem after I got off the Mattapan trolley station. I happened to sit down next to this elderly woman. She, like most people that sees the kindness through me, began to have a dialogue with me. I think she was telling me about how the roads from the trolley to Mattapan has changed over the years. We pass houses and streets along the way. Each newly built house brought back some fond memories for her. I never said much to her but rather just listened to what she was saying out of respect to an elderly person. When I got home, I got inspired to write this poem from her perspective. I decided to put myself in her shoes maybe 50 years ago and think about how times have changed and what she has observed over the years. I thought it would be a fascinating way for me to write this poem. Her unique point of view was valuable to me as we road from the CVS stop all the way to Mattapan Square. The poem's genre is to be read from the voice of an old lady. I recall how elderly people tend to repeat themselves over and over again. So I kept the repetition of "Oh how times have changed" throughout the poem to reflect that persona. Also I left out the correct spelling of past tense words to reflect how much education she may have gotten in her heydays.

"The Silent Fight Within"

If you really had a chance to know the life story of Mrs. Marva J. Stanton, you would agree that she is a fighter and a very stubborn woman to say the least who refused to call it quits when at times the doctors did not have any hope of her living past the age of seventeen. Mrs. Stanton became my mother in law in 2008 and I got to learn about Sickle Cell from my wife's stories of her life's battle for survival. Mrs. Stanton is truly a one of a kind story of overcoming the odds against her. So on her sixty-second birthday my wife wanted to celebrate her life's journey which no one could have believed it to be possible at birth that she would live to see sixty plus years.

In turn I wanted to write a poem to symbolize her fight with Sickle Cell disease. I wrote this poem from her perspective and in her own voice as an old woman giving a speech to a hospital filled with other children with Sickle Cell. I also wanted to emphasize the silent fight of her battle within in contrast to the days when I was in school reading about the Scarlet Letter. That book resonated in my mind and heart as I was writing this poem. So I wrote the second poem with the notation that my mother-in-law too had a secret letter "S" that was hidden in her bosom.

For many years, I had listened to my mother-in-law's concerns about getting tested but never would I have guessed that I would be a carrier of the trait. It turns out that in the Haitian culture, we are carriers of the Sickle Cell trait in our blood line. However the odds are rare for us to ever have the full blown disease. So on that day of my test results, her worries were proven right that the odds of my wife and I having a healthy child would be slim. But today with the proper education and the improvement in scientific research for a cure, we are hopeful that she will live to be a grandma one day.

For all those who suffer from Sickle Cell disease, I dedicate this poem to you and your *Silent Fight Within*.

"A Warrior within Sixty-Three Rounds"

This poem was an on chore to "The Silent Fight Within" after having taken a poetry workshop by Tom Daley in Cambridge. People loved it so much but felt she was missing some characters that needed to be developed. A few weeks later as I was talking to my fiancé at that time, the poem came to me; in less than two hours the gist of the poem was done. Prior to that I was not sure where I wanted to go with her character. I felt that her story was complete from the first poem. I also did not want to take away from the built up of her character as a strong woman. I did not want to go into her life struggle and make her sound weak. So I was at a standstill of how I wanted her to be seen. I kept in my mind that this poem was about celebrating her achievements and not taking away from it or having people feel sorry for her.

Therefore when it came to writing a second round about her life I not only describe the pain she went through but I included the people who have been in her life all these years. Those who have seen her as a child to that of a grown woman, and now in her primal age of retirement. This second poem is a tribute to them. For not given up on her throughout the years. On her sixty-fourth birthday, I presented to my mother-in-law both completed poems in a plaque. The original one was given to the nurses to hang at The Carney Hospital in Dorchester, Massachusetts since Mrs. Stanton had been a fixture in that hospital for most of her life.

"Brother Man"

Brother Man, like the poem is a one of a kind person that you meet once in a blue moon as they say. I was inspired to write this poem base off a character that I use to see on my way in to work just every other day. The man is somewhat related to my wife come to find out weeks later after writing this poem. But I never spoke to him at all. What I did was observe his behavior. And the best way to describe his behavior was from the cartoon character of *Fat Albert and the Cosby Kids* from back in the day. Here was a man that walked with a swagger to him, lackadaisical and nonchalant as if he had not a worry in the world. He was truly a happy go lucky kind of a guy.

I watched him for months as he use to walk ahead of me most times to my bus stop. Once in a while we would give each other that proverbial head wave as a sign of respect and recognition of each other but we never spoke to one another. Than one day, he came to mind in my Lyric poetry class that I was in as my teacher began to read one of his poems. He had a great voice for the character that he wrote about in his poem. The poem was a mixture of African American slang talk and hip-hop. I was in amazement the way he illustrated that poem that I began to visualize what this character would look like in person. And the brother that I saw on my way to work came to mind as who this potential character in that poem would look like. So that night I was inspired to write a similar poem like my teacher's about this Brother Man that I kept seeing in my neighborhood.

I imagine him to be a funny character with all the smooth words that would attract a lady as if I had already presumed with his swagger and all that he must be a lady's man. A brother with all the right rhymes in his vocabulary. The poem is truly a play on the 70s lifestyle with a twist of a 21st century brother going to work to take care of his bills.

In the process of writing Brother Man, I had a vision of what direction that I wanted to take the poem in itself. But along the journey as you can see was the life of Brother Man, I changed the tone to be that of a surprisingly religious man. And I think the change was due to being in a christian atmosphere which compelled me not to make him turn out to be a regular thug in the streets trying to hustle to make ends meet. I changed his character around to have a positive outlook on life base on how I described him to be. A hard working man doing his thing. There was no reason to shut down his game since few brothers in the streets ever make an attempt to get up so early in the morning to do the right thing. And I felt I needed to leave that positive feel and surprise twist to the poem.

FREDERIQUE Media Productions

Made in the USA
Charleston, SC
14 December 2012